Contents

Who Were the

P irates have been sailing the high seas and stealing from towns and ships for centuries. But where did the cut-throat business of piracy start?

SCANDINAVIAN SCARERS

Vikings from Scandinavia terrorized Europe from the 8th century AD. They were fearless warriors with a reputation for fighting and stealing.

VIKING WEAPONS

The Vikings used lots of weapons, including short swords and axes. One of their greatest weapons was the longship. It was very light and moved quickly through water. This made carrying out *raids* much easier. It also meant they could also escape quickly!

UP CLOSE

PIRATES

PAUL HARRISON

W
FRANKLIN WATTS
LONDON·SYDNEY

Published in 2008 by Franklin Watts
Reprinted in 2010

Copyright © 2008 Arcturus Publishing Limited

Franklin Watts
338 Euston Road
London NW1 3BH

Franklin Watts Australia
Level 17/207 Kent Street
Sydney NSW 2000

Author: Paul Harrison
Designer (new edition): Silvie Rabbe
Editor (new edition): Fiona Tulloch

Picture credits: Bridgeman Art Library: page 16, bottom left; Corbis: title page; page 5; page 19, top and bottom right; Chris Collingwood: front cover and page 14; Indy Magnoli: page 21, bottom right; Kobal Collection: page 2, page 7, bottom right, page 8, page 9, top and bottom right, page 12, bottom left, page 13, top and bottom, page 15, top and middle, page 20, top right, page 21, top right; Mary Evans: page 7, top left, page 20, bottom left; Reuters: page 18, bottom left; The Art Archive: page 12, middle right, page 24; Topfoto: page 10, bottom, page 11, bottom right, page 15, bottom right.

A CIP catalogue record for this book is available from the British Library

Dewey number: 364.16'4

ISBN: 978-1-4451-0128-6
SL000946EN

Printed in China

Franklin Watts is a division of Hachette Children's Books, an Hachette UK Company
www.hachette.co.uk.

Pirates?

GOLDEN YEARS
The first pirates of the Caribbean were French hunters, called buccaneers. They fought lots of wars against the Spanish. The "golden age" of piracy was from the late 1600s to the early 1700s.

DRESSED TO KILL
Vikings didn't wear much armour because they needed to be light on their feet. A few chose to wear helmets to protect their heads.

Legal Piracy

When is a pirate not a pirate? The answer is when he is a privateer—a sailor given permission to act like a pirate.

CORSAIRS

Although most pirates came from the Caribbean, the North African seas were home to pirates known as "corsairs". They captured people for ransom or sold them as slaves.

Sailors were so scared of pirates that they often surrendered without a fight!

PERMISSION TO STEAL

A "letter of marque" was a *permit* given to ships by a king or queen. It allowed captains to steal from their enemy during wars. Sir Francis Drake was a famous privateer.

6

DAILY RISKS

Pirates were often injured by all the fighting and shooting they did. Sometimes they were hurt by falling masts or collapsed *rigging*. Injured pirates usually worked as ships' cooks.

JUSTICE

Pirates who were caught were put on trial by the government. Most trials were short and ended in death. The executions were really gory and happened in public to put people off becoming pirates.

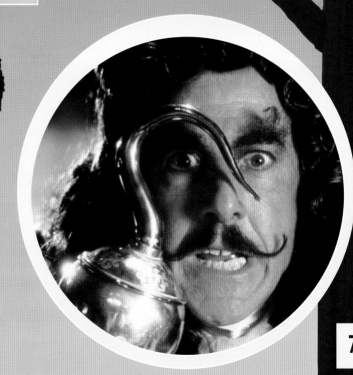

Myth vs Reality

E veryone knows something about pirates, such as what they looked like or what they got up to. How much of what you know is true—and how much is made up?

WHO'S A PRETTY BOY THEN?

Just like in the movies, parrots were favourite pirate pets. This is because they could be taught to speak and were entertaining. Pet monkeys were also popular.

DIVING BOARD ———

Pirates never actually made their prisoners walk the plank. It would have been simpler just to throw them overboard!

LAW-ABIDING CITIZENS?

Even though most people think pirates were *lawless* thieves, many pirates lived by the pirate code. This meant that they followed rules, such as voting on how to share treasure out and agreeing not to fight each other.

Pirates didn't bury treasure, which means they didn't have treasure maps.

Pirate Essentials

What did a pirate need during the golden age of piracy? There were a few things that a buccaneer couldn't do without.

GET THE POINT

Some of the most common weapons were short, sharp swords. Pirates also used clubs and axes.

BANG!

The flintlock pistol was a pirate favourite. These were lightweight and easily available. They got their name from the piece of flint that was used to light the gunpowder to fire the shot.

The famous cutlass sword wasn't common until after the golden age of piracy.

SECOND HOME

Pirates needed places to spend their stolen fortunes. Towns like Port Royal in Jamaica and the island of New Providence became pirate hideaways.

SHIVER ME TIMBERS

Most pirates used small quick boats known as sloops, rather than large, heavily armed boats which needed a large crew to run them.

Treasure

People became pirates for lots of different reasons. They might have been on the run from a crime, wanted to sail the seas, or just liked stealing. They all had one aim though—to get as rich as possible!

BITS AND PIECES

The most important coins were the gold doubloon and the silver peso, which was called a "piece of eight". It was worth eight reales—a lower value Spanish coin.

BURIED TREASURE

Pirates didn't really bury their treasure—they didn't keep it for long enough! They usually spent it on drinking and gambling.

BLACK BART

The most successful pirate was nicknamed "Black Bart". In one raid alone, he captured a Portuguese ship and took its valuable cargo—over 90,000 gold coins and priceless jewels.

A law in 1717 allowed pirates to keep their treasure if they promised to give up pirating.

CHEEKY CHAPPIES

In 1716 around 300 pirates raided a Spanish camp, where the sailors were searching for their treasure after a storm. Instead, the pirates found the treasure, making off with nearly 350,000 pieces of eight!

Famous Pirates

M ost of the tales about piracy came about because of well-known pirates. Here are some of the most famous ones.

STRIKE A LIGHT

Edward Teach, or "Blackbeard", was the most famous pirate of all. He had a wild beard and used to stick lit candles in his hat when in battle. He also wore belts across his chest, stuffed with pistols.

During the 1200s there was a pirate known as the Black Monk. He was a real monk!

ANYTHING YOU CAN DO

Mary Read and Anne Bonny were two of the most famous female pirates. They were caught in 1720 but escaped hanging by being pregnant.

HAVE A HEART

Francois l'Olonnais was a bloodthirsty pirate. He had a reputation for torturing and murdering his prisoners. He once ate the heart of one of his captives.

RUM FELLOW

Captain Henry Morgan was so famous that there is a rum named after him. He was a privateer who retired rich, though some people think he was really a pirate.

Battles on the

P irates fought long and hard to get their treasure. Only the toughest pirates survived the fierce battles.

DARK LEGEND

Samuel Bellamy, or "Black Sam", was a pirate for less than a year. He worked with Blackbeard, capturing more than fifty ships before he was killed aged 29.

GETTING CROSS

In the 1515, Pier Gerlofs Donia and his fearsome crew captured 28 Dutch ships. He became known as "The Cross of the Dutchmen".

Seas

OPPORTUNISTS

Pirates didn't have ships built especially for them. They had to equip their ships with things they had looted. Sometimes it was easy—they would just steal an entire ship!

> Pirates didn't just steal treasure—they also stole food, medicine and clothes.

GUNS

The gunner of a ship was an important crew member. He would aim the cannon and his men would load and fire it.

Dangerous

Although the golden age of piracy finished nearly 300 years ago, pirates still exist today. Little has changed in certain parts of the seas.

HOSED OFF

Pirate attacks are common near Malaysia. Recently, a Japanese cargo vessel was attacked here. The brave crew chased the pirates away—with high-pressure water hoses!

HUNTED DOWN

Malaysia, Singapore and Indonesia have a *fleet* of ships patrolling the nearby Malacca Straits. This area is popular with modern-day pirates because it is one of the busiest shipping lanes in the world.

Although pirates still exist, your chances of ever meeting a one are very small.

MODERN MENACE

Pirates from Somalia sell stolen goods on the black market.

NEW WEAPONS

Instead of flintlock pistols and sloops, modern-day pirates use machine guns and motorboats. However, most of today's pirates are very poor, so they chase boats with clubs and *machetes*—just like pirates of the golden age.

Entertaining

M ost of the pictures of pirates we have in our heads come from films, stories and paintings. They're great entertainment, but how accurate are they?

MOVIES

Captain Jack Sparrow in the *Pirates of the Caribbean* films is witty, charming and good-looking—most real pirates were the complete opposite!

REAL WRITING

A book called *A General History of the Robbings and Murders of the Most Notorious Pirates* tells the life stories of a number of different pirates. Experts believe the stories are true.

Pirates

Most of the drawings you see of pirates are by Victorian illustrators.

THE CLASSIC

In *Treasure Island*, Long John Silver looks for buried treasure marked on a map by a big cross. He has a peg leg too!

PIRATE SONGS

In 1879 Gilbert and Sullivan wrote a comic opera called *The Pirates of Penzance*. Piracy became *romanticized* during the Victorian period.

Glossary

FLEET
A group of ships sailing together for the same purpose.

LAWLESS
Operating outside of the law.

MACHETE
A broad knife often used as a weapon.

PERMIT
An official document giving someone permission to do something.

RAID
A sudden attack or assault, often involving theft.

RIGGING
An apparatus attached to the hull of a ship in order to make the boat move as a whole. It includes cordage, sails, and masts.

ROMANTICIZE
To make something seem better than it really is or was.

Further Reading

Caribbean Pirates: A Treasure Chest of Fact, Ficiton and Folklore
George Beahm, Hampton Roads Publishing Co., 2007

Pirate (DK Eye Witness Books)
Richard Platt, DK Children 2004

Pirates
John Matthews, Athenium, 2006

The Best Book of Pirates
Barnaby Howard, Kingfisher, 2006

The Book of Pirates
Howard Pyle, Dover Publications, 2007

The History of Pirates
Angus Konstam, The Lyons Press, 2002

Index